Dedicated to:

Paris and Ellie our two beautiful daughters who are at the core of our life. Family means everything and because of these two we wake up each morning excited to see what they have for us. From musical performances to home cooked meals they always brighten our day.

Please send your insightful feedback to us:
Twitter: @BijanNas
Facebook: @Entrepreneurroadmap
Website: Everydayisnewday.com

Introduction

Now that I finally decided to write a book I have to admit that it actually feels great; it is almost like an achievement. I remember when I was 11 years old, my sister took me to the national library, I am not sure if she chose it for me, or if I picked it up but the first ever novel I read was *The Call of the Wild* by Jack London. Still to this day I get goosebumps when I think back of its chapters. Everything flashbacks right in front of my eyes: the tenacity to fight for your life, the sadness and horror, a white snow blanket sometimes covered with drops of blood, and an adventurous life. I admire Jack so much in how he could write a story from a dog's worldview so emotionally present and vivid. Even for me as Persian preteen boy on other side of the world with a completely different cultural upbringing I was able to connect and feel it inside and out. Like the cold breeze of north pole in my face – which was unimaginable in my middle eastern city. The joy and excitement of life, sound of the wild as angry wolves, mesmerizing colors of approaching sunsets and unusual drive to stay alive come to mind when I think of this novel. Not to forget the ever so prominent message of never giving up in spite of all adversity that life throws at you.

Now that Persian teenager who fell in love with a Canadian story is in his fifties and lives in Vancouver, Canada. Is this the laws of attraction? I think so. It is like in the movies; somehow a book I read in 1980 is connected to this very moment for me.

It is not usual to see a retired physician who has spent almost two decades working with homeless drug users around the world write a book on entrepreneurship. But here we are in the land of opportunity in North America. As a little kid, I always heard about the American dream (Iran was a USA ally at the time). You have to do what you love and finally I am here and do not have any legitimate reasons for excuses not to pursue my dream. Even if you want to hang on to those excuses, reality is: no one cares.

Why Entrepreneurs and Why a Roadmap?

I chose entrepreneurs because I admire people who think differently and have the desire to make a positive impact in the world. They seem to always have an inner voice pulling them to change things for the better and creating peace and harmony. Why roadmap? Because as an emigrant who traveled all the way from Iran to come to the end of the world (West End), I came with the purpose and ambition to achieve everything I had not been able to fulfill. With the excitement of new beginning your inner voice tells you: You will make it. You will create your own little world and build everything that you didn't have a chance to make.

What is the translation? To get lured into the attractive world of entrepreneurship; the journey of building your own business to explore, create, build and build and build. But oh man, you can't see the real story behind the scene. It is shocking how much support, mentorship, and guts it takes to go over the ups and downs. Not to forget the tremendous degree of mental and physical toughness that is required.

In this path, it's not unusual to get exposed to many false hopes and promises like being lured into "Get Rich Quick" scheme platforms that seem very promising from the start but very soon you will be left alone and dry. In that situation try to make sense of everything that happen to you. You are in total frustration and confusion on what is going on, constantly asking yourself what has been your fault, what did you do wrong to deserve this?

You keep reminding yourself: I swear to God that I have positive intentions and great plans to create, as well as amazing products and services to offer. But guess what? Apparently, that is the destiny all entrepreneurs have to go through to test their tenacity, endurance and faith.

Most of us (as emigrants) have a strong desire to succeed especially when you look back to where you left off, what a nightmare you've been through. In most countries of origin not even having the basic rights like cave man rights: right to dress right to eat and right to laugh!

All those memories will keep you upbeat and thinking of quitting is the last thing it comes to your mind. Living in the most beautiful place with all the blessings around you, wonderful souls, inspiring cultures, abundance in almost everything, the only thing that you need to know is your roadmap! Aha now you see where did we get to this title, an intrinsic intense desire to be a game changer and be a people of our dreams but at the same time confused on where we are heading. As immigrants, we wanted to contribute a new abbreviation to North American vocabulary. To pay our dues me and Lucy coined the phrase USL as "Universal Simple Language" for entrepreneurs! Also, as you see we politely put a social media "handle" to say how up to date and contemporary we are!

Welcome to:

@EntrepreneurRoadmap

Chapter 1

Everything started from a beautiful day of April 2006 in Vancouver (first time I ever traveled to Canada) that I was invited to give a short presentation on project we've been working on. It was designed for homeless drug users in Tehran Iran with the support of several organizations for years. In those projects, we were offering a variety of services from food to HIV prevention needle package. After my wonderful inspiring speech, I decided to rent a bike and go around Stanley park and right there I fell in love with this city and its surroundings, the beach, perfect spring like weather and sun. When I'm hearing daily conversation, I look at people and think: don't even start complaining about rain as I'm a rain lover! Want to know why, just travel around the world and you'll see folks literally praying for weeks to get few drops of rain into their dry lands.

Back in Iran I remember one day I got a phone a call from a translator that a journalist from Yahoo is interested to have an interview with you about work you guy's doings as it seems against the odd and progressive for an oppressive regime. As always we have been delighted to see international experts to learn from them and at the same time get exposure to the outside world. I said a big yes and asked him to drop by. Soon after I realised that I have the pleasure of having Kevin Sites with his cool camera connecting to internet in our center! I felt like being in CNN reporting documentaries right in the middle of battlefield. Later on, he put his report in a book called Hot Zone: (http://www.kevinsitesreports.com/in-the-hot-zone/) just for some of you who are curios about my background and crazy stuff we were up to back in 2000.

Now that I'm going back almost 15 years ago and read his report, it gives me a surreal feeling, a mix of achievement and pride, an honor of opportunity that God gave me to be among hundreds of homeless folks connecting with them, offer them food and medical supplies, learn from them, get inspired every single day and become who I am today. Working with folks that most frequent encounter in their life has been either an early morning kick in their butt to go away from that store front or a police raid in back alley and dragging their disheveled exhausted body to the police van sending them off to jail.

The first lesson in entrepreneurship journey is to have an intense desire for change something that bothers you and you believe in it from bottom of your heart; no matter how much naysayers are trying to prove you otherwise but you know, that you have answer for it.

We may want to call it "passion", which probably is the most important driving force that generate enough enthusiasm for you to go against all odds. To open first official needle exchange program in the country and living under a fundamentalist theocratic regime which is against almost everything as whole world is their enemy unless proven otherwise, you have to be either stunt master or don't care about what will happen next. We opened a holistic treatment center caring for HIV positive injection drug users, offering needle exchange program which basically is getting their dirty needles and give them a clean unused one to prevent sharing with other users. This will stop spread of all kinds of infections

I guess simply because you see that this is the last chance for you in this life as far as your aspirations and high hopes and dreams concerns, to make it or break it. I hear in this part of the world, for individuals to become excited about entrepreneurship, one of the main well tolerated chants is to look down at what you do as an employee. The speaker rant always echoes the so called getting out the rat race vicious cycle which in my belief is a disgrace to all amazing brave souls, the men and women out there who put their life and energy at stake to make this world a better place as a firefighter, as a nurse, as a janitor and so on and so forth.

I don't think to make people excited about getting involve in business and entrepreneurship which I believe every singe individual in this world have that potential, you have to play the blame and shame game against the most amazing hard working souls that basically running the whole town. It's lame, makes me throw up. If it wasn't because of all emergency room staff work, your kids were dead and your city because of all those loyal dedicated workers would have been a pile of garbage and no shiny entrepreneurs have been volunteer to jump in the middle of a fire explosion to save that little girl's life.

Thus, you wonderful mentors and leaders shut up and rewrite your speech especially when you're in the big conventions on the stage pumped up with applause of thousands of audiences who are looking up to you as a strong leader. Speak life and praise God or whoever you believe in which has given you a 2nd chance. Why 2nd chance because as a classic story most successful entrepreneurs have actually been the master of screw up in their life, because there is no any other way to learn things.

Most common cycle of change

Pic 1

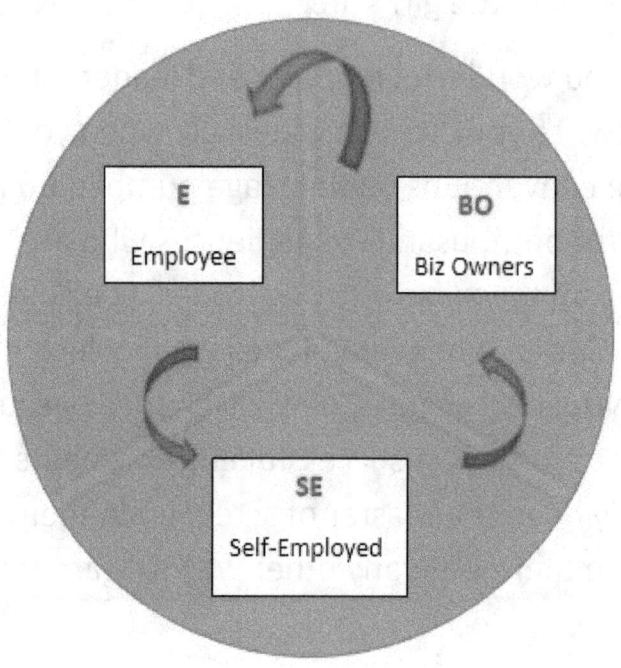

I believe strongly that the first sign that you are going to become a successful real entrepreneur is not to get caught into your little success bubble. You've to be able to appreciate that big part of your success is not yours, it comes from countless hours of work of other team members around you (which we tend not to see that) who supported you along the way to get where you are today.

Respect for others is the first none negotiating quality of a true entrepreneur, respecting yourself and respecting others, appreciating yourself and others, having the highest human quality called gratitude. As you see in above infographic, every compartment has separated by a line or wall which define the barriers you have to overcome when you move from one phase to another. Among main barriers to move from Employee part to Self-Employed are fear of not being good enough to take care of your business (perfectionism), low confidence and self steam. The later usually goes back to your past or current environment which is not very nurturing and empowering. But remember most of the time there is nothing wrong with you, it's your perception that speaks to you and made you feel less or more. I always refer it to 2 little angel and Devil cartoons characters over your right and left shoulder which one (the devil) talking you out of being at your best and do things and the other one (the angel) encourage you to be the Samaritan, the good guy.

If you feel you are not good enough it's because somebody down the road has told you so, which most of the time it's your close friend or your family members or significant others which believe it or not they do it without negative intention. But because it is a close friend, a relative etc, their suggestion does resonate with you and stays in your head for rest of your life. Because we tend to believe what our beloved friends and family members are telling us is the truth; as they love us they should be right.

Anyway, enough of bashing close friends and families, all that I want to say here is that if you will be able to sit down in a quite space without any distraction, and focus on real true yourself and erasing all those past and present filters, then you'll see that you are nothing but a powerful amazing source of energy that God created you to thrive not to survive.

Chapter 2

I remember somebody said world is running on shoulder of bunch of stupid doers as all smart over thinkers are either busy thinking or criticising those stupid's! Many things happen by accident I agree at least that's what we assume. Part of this is because most of us haven't been raised learning "law of attraction". When we see the so-called accident happens, we tend to forget about the fact that it's up to you and me to turn around those "accidents" or good luck or bad luck to something purposefully amazing that later in life become our destiny, our great project and our gift to the world. We tend to forget that we have the power of pushing or not pushing the final trigger.

Thus, don't tell me he or she is lucky or got there by chance, as you basically tent to excuse yourself out of law of universe. As a rule, always go back to iceberg phenomenon and remember that those Olympic athletes works their butt off for 4 to 8 years for that 2 minutes of achievement and glory. 2 minutes is the tip of iceberg and 4 to 8 years is underwater that we tend not pay attention to.

As I was growing up during post Shah era I was bombarded with tons of scientific documentaries because under Islamic regime the only movies we were allowed to watch were either scientific films or Chinese marshal art by Bruce Lee or Jackie Chan (good for them) as policy of no sex no laughter no life was the dominant atmosphere over all media platforms! As a child, I grew up with hundreds of movies like life of Thomas Edison and torment of Galileo which ironically being tortured by the church! Those stories had a tremendous effect on building my mindset about who I am today and what I always wanted to create.

I remember that as soon as I got to medical university one day I took a pen and paper and started to write about my future and showed it to my sister which was 5 years older than me. I can't remember exact words but it was something along these lines: one day I'll become a scientist, going to the top of the mountain like the way I saw Mohammad Abdus Salam as my idol the winner of noble prize in physics was sitting in one of photos in his office. Why him because his plan was to open a scholarship program for third world country talented individuals to attend a university in Trist of Italy but conditional to give him a guarantee that they will go back to their own country and serve their people after they finish their degree. I loved the way that those smart people like him carry a heart of a champion and were not fooled by their higher IQ or badges to forget about their root, where they come from and their calling. One of the ways to believe how amazing of a human being you are is to go back to your memory and bring all those hopes and dream plans that one day you were %100 sure you'll achieve it. Bring them out of your mind's deepest tunnels and put it right in front of your eyes and be proud of yourself. This is your real you who had great aspirations and thoughts many years ago as one day will change the world for the better and we are all have it, it's nothing belong to specific group of people, you just have to find yours. One of the reasons me and my wife Lucy created the infographic of Fortune Hand is to have a checklist of do-es and do-n'ts on a daily basis, make sure it'll keep you upbeat during the course of the day especially as an entrepreneur who don't know what life events will through at you as the day goes by.

Fortune hand

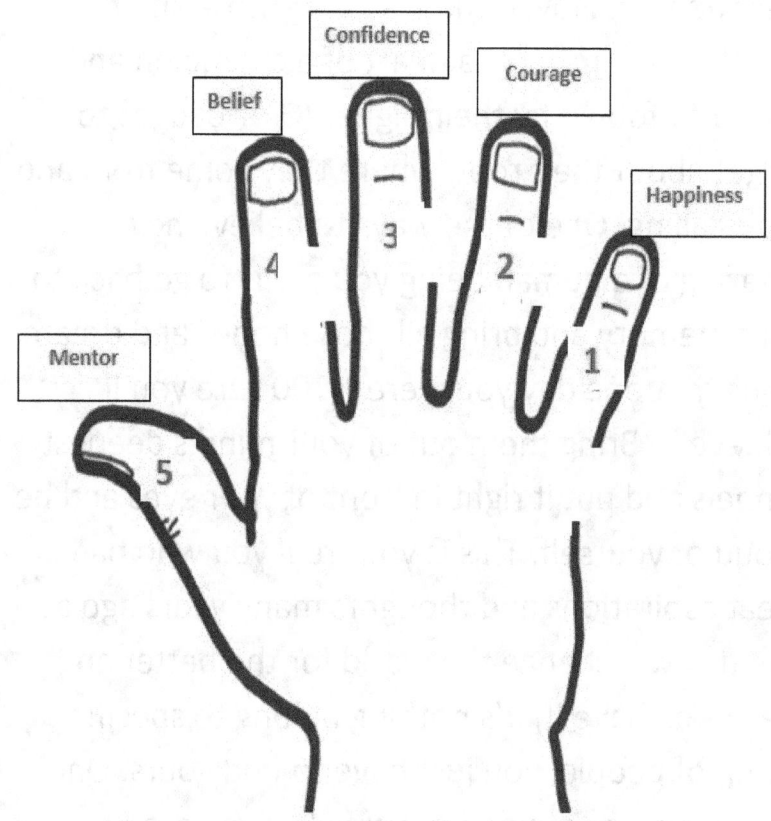

As you see here the first rule of the game to become fortunate is: to be happy. For you to be happy you need to have balance.

The concept of having balance in your life always was fascinating me, especially when I was trying to get to the bottom of Chinese Yin and Yang circle which made me dizzy by just looking at it and at the end wasn't getting anything, sorry no offence for all my amazing Namaste friends! Because of that I was trying hard to put it in a simple way, be able to explain it to my 2 beautiful teenage daughters, because there is an old say that if you'll be able to explain anything to a child you have learned it yourself!

I knew that Lucy has been talking about points of chakra but it was too much for me and was going over my head. After all I wasn't raised in a culture of energy and universe so far and so forth, I was a medical Dr for God sake. But at the same time, I had to explain the ultimate meaning of state of balance to myself and to my daughters. Surprise surprise I used human anatomy as my background education that I can relate to as this is deepest that I can go! Out of that I created 5 points of balance that you have to feed them all, to make sure you are achieving your basic state of balance:

Your 5 points of Balance

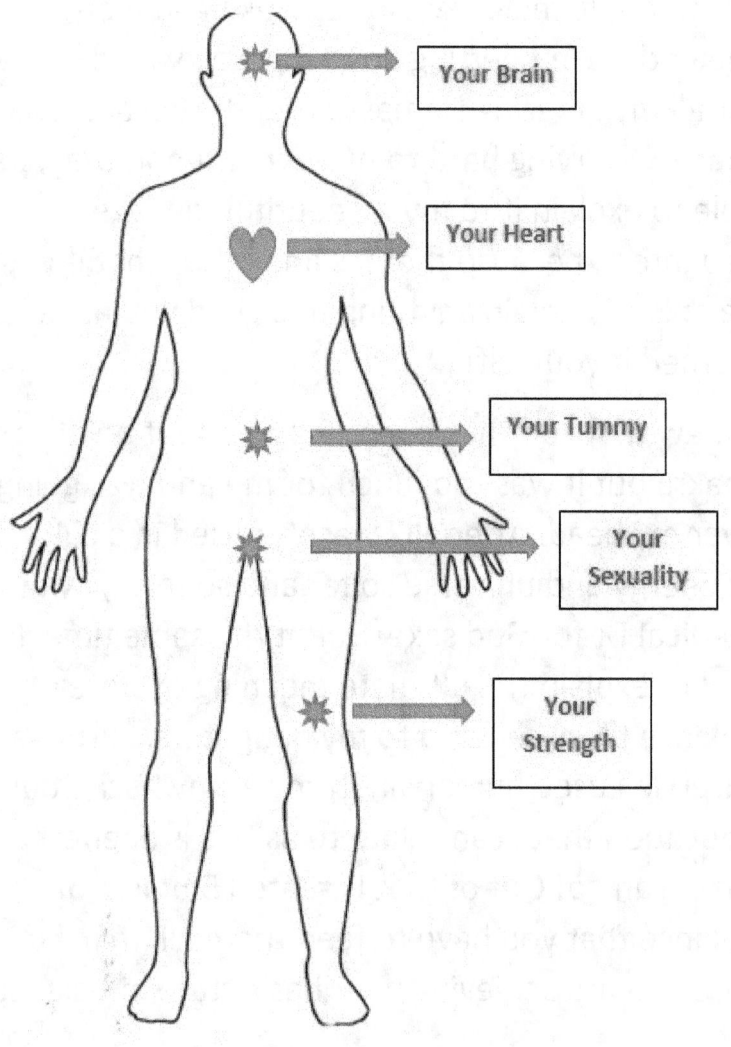

Your Brain

Your Heart

Your Tummy

Your Sexuality

Your Strength

No 1 is your brain (reading books, going to college etc.) to make sure you don't feel you're dumb. The other way is to become street smart and feed your brain by learning from life. Feeding your brain where I come from is an obsession as a Persian or like Chinese family who's their children have to pursue the highest level of academic achievement. I've seen middle class families who put their life at stake to cut down on almost everything they could and redirect all their resources to make sure their wonderful kids go to college or university of choice. In this commotion (day and night private tutors and transport their talented kids here and there) there is no conversation about how in the world do you feel about your future or: sweetheart what do you want to be when you are a grown up. Forget it, it is what it is; either you like or not. Usually your parent and your dominant culture dictate what you've to pursue not what you love to become or to do. The major metrics that have been used in this horrible scenario is the social status and income you can make. Your feelings or emotions are the last and least important things to talk about it, they don't have any place in this equation.

Feeding your brain like read one book a week, listen or watch audio and videos about personal growth, gaining technical skills on top of your academic badges are all ways we want to make sure we are up to our highest standards. But make sure that it shouldn't be at the expense of loosing your sanity and become a Brainiac.

No 2 is your heart and soul by doing meditation, religion practices and prayers, mindfulness, yoga, 5ht dimension of energy and universe, whatever, etc to soften your souls and understand the definition of gratitude and compassion. We've all seen the effect of cold hearted human being who failed to feed their soul and spirit, and end result is a very intelligent being but definitely not a human being.

No 3 is literally all about your tummy and what you consume. I borrowed it from Chinese proverb I guess that it says you are what you eat, nothing about centre of universe nothing about those weird definitions, just you are what you eat. It resonates with my background in addiction medicine as I witnessed that people are what they eat, what they drink, what they smoke and you know the rest! In today fast food era and widespread complications like Diabetes type 2 among teenagers, heart disease, obesity and hundreds of newly born sicknesses of 21sth century, it is an inevitable manifestation of you are what you consume.

No 4 is your sexuality and I didn't get it from Adam and Eve but by having encountered many couples during my counselling sessions as a family physician. I was hearing over and over again that their relationship was going down the drain just by not having a nurturing sex life. After a while they became a horrible brother and sister and why horrible because the agreement was screwed up as from what it was originally supposed to be. It dropped down as a soulmate and sexmate and everything mate all the way to a brother and sister which is a blood driven contract that you will inherit it and there is no way out of it (for you guys out there that are not enjoying a very happy relationship with your brother and sisters).

Just look at clichés men's beer times and women sisterhood club which somehow is all about no sexlife relationships as the only main trigger. When you watch them talking and behaving so nasty and rude and gossipy (both men and women) you easily can see the cover up for their insecurities of failed sex life. I don't want to pretend that I'm a sex expert but for the sake of life if you don't have a good nurturing sex (ask your sex therapist about it) consider it an alarming sign that bigger storm to appear anytime soon in your marriage horizon.

No 5 last but not least is the whole movement and fitness notion and getting out of your couch potato lifestyle. Somehow movement creates amazing arrays of hormonal and chemical release in your body that has no competitor like it. It makes you feel strong in all aspects of your mind and souls and gives you high energy and so on. It's not surprising to see the surge of walking consultation or walking meetings these days as movement is the master of all healthy behaviors.

I have seen when kids who are stuck with their phone or boys with their game for hours and you see everything will change in their body, their attitude, their eating habit, their energy level, their concentration and many more.

This was just the factor number one in Fortune hand "Happiness" which Lucy taught me to apply as the first and most important rule to start strong for the day.

I have to admit that being with Lucy as my 2nd marriage was a start of a healing process for a man coming a long way from a war torn Middle East. When I was 10 years old Islamic revolution came to town and I remember one day before the previous regime collapse, I was walking with my dad in one of the busiest traditional shopping mal called Bazar and asking him: dad do you think that all those rumors about regime change is true and he was telling me with %100 confidence: Son do you think that the King (Shah) with all of his stronghold army and infrastructure will fall apart in one day! With all my surprise right in front of my eyes the next day the national radio was occupied by revolutionary militia and they declared new government, as at that time we didn't have YouTube or other social media platforms!

That was the start of a ticking clock for me to witness all the killings and fights and on top of that 8 years of war with neighbour country that left one million casualties and tons of painful memories which made Vietnam and US war just another movie for us. Fast forward to the day that I proposed to Lucy she started the most amazing healing process without even knowing which took a long time and it was really worth it. I got my real life back. The journey started by her showing me the movie Secret! You can guess my reaction, she either is one of those crazy illusionists that believe in palm reading or is a cult religion follower etc etc! But these are all defence mechanisms I adopted as a man who has been living constantly under survival mode as everything from lunatic Islamic government to the corrupt city hall office are against you. You constantly carrying the armour of paranoia, bitterness and fear with you and very soon before you even realise they become a part of who you are.

Chapter 3

There are certain things in life not worth of procrastination; things like saying I love you to your soulmate, thank you to your mom and dad, appreciate your neighbour for his/her act of kindness and list goes on and on. Being raised in a war-torn region and become a volunteer in a logistic war back up hospital since I was 13 years old taught me that "life is short" is for real, it's not a joke and you have only one shot in this life not 2 not 3 even though that miracles happen for some of us getting 2nd or 3rd chance out of life and death circumstance or become a cancer survivor or other inspiring stories. But overall life is awesome and so precious to take it lightly. On the other hand, your conscience and samaritan tendency pushes you to sacrifice for higher causes like your family, your country, your belief etc. and it can go to the extreme which could almost blind you. If you don't have a good grip on It'll tip you over to the so-called sacred syndrome either as a gang member that cut your skin and give some drops of blood under oath of brotherhood or blow yourself up in a mall because you have been brain washed that you are fighting with Devils. Thus, watch out when you play in the field of conscience as there are plenty of weird folks and doctrines out there that can lure you into all kinds of cults driven movement.

Lucy once asked a wise old woman that if she can give her a last word of wisdom, what it would be and she smiled graciously and said: don't take yourself seriously!

Speak life to others and uplift them as an employer, leader, mentor, manager, and a human being. You will be amazed that word of praise, appreciation and love goes extra miles and is more powerful than any tactical phrase that you have learned during your leadership school.

I believe you are what you think and the rest is just noise. I don't want to be your motivational speaker and definitely isn't my purpose to pump you up with no solid foundation behind it, but believe me there is only one and only one top expert in your life that can clearly see who you are and what are you capable of and it's nobody other than you.

To make it more dramatic we've created the RR factor as Regret Ruler! You've heard about bucket list or do what you love and I'm trying to give you another push by using your regret ruler to measure yours every single day, make sure in scale of zero to 10 you're getting closer to zero as living your life. When you walk beside cemetery you can hear all deep ahh sounds, message from the grave that caused us all a great deal of disappointment. To be behind so much in so many things they supposed to do; in song you supposed to sing, in technology to be created, in world justice to fight for and so on. If they would've been able to measure it for every single individual right before he/she hit the grave, you'll get a pretty much idea what am I talking about.

Just don't be one of them. I feel like the woodoos in the movies that hypnotizing the audience but in a nutshell, don't wait for perfect time to do what you love because maybe tomorrow is too late.

Power of words are among the most amazing miracles that you can use or abuse it during your daily interactions with your colleagues and customers. You will be amazed that just a simple change in word of "why" to "how" totally shift a paradigm; a judgmental phrase to a sympathizing one. The origin of words usually come from our preoccupations about people and events even before they open their mouth or do anything; we call it "first impression". If you imagine that during the day we carry 100 thoughts 90 of them are having connection down deep into our subconscious level of mind. They are usually hard to get access to in terms of been able to analyse your behavior and finding answers why did I do that or why did I say that. The more you become conscious of your subconscious (Lucy's quote) the better you are off in making a great decision and impression in others.

By no surprise that as part of our business coaching we have a practice called power of the words and audience see it as one of the eye-opening exercises which not only affect their daily interaction with customers but also the quality of family and friend's one.

I called it filters of our personality. We have been raised by all those filters that our family our religion our books and movies our significant others have inoculated into our brains. Most of the time without even knowing what are they doing and what kind of effect it'll bring into us later in our life but most of them have long-lasting effect in our character and attitude.

To understand the concept of filters consider them as different glasses we wear during the day, the pity glasses, the sexist glasses, the father glasses, the bully glasses or the victim glasses. They all will affect the way we look at the world and people around us without knowing the fact that we're having glasses on (refer to a busy father who yell at the poor family members asking who has replaced my glasses and the awkward moment that little daughter point at his head).

This is the closest I can get to explain the effect of our thoughts that are deep rooted in our subconscious. It doesn't mean you always unaware which actually is an excuse for another practice called self observation and self awareness but it simply tells us be careful about those intense judgmental beliefs that you carry on and thinking it's written on stone simply because your family upbringing says so!

Thanks to Canadian influence today that I can understand the concept of cross cultural tolerance in its deepest sense. I always say to my daughters that even though that there is a norm to think American are the bravest because they all sing under one flag and when they do they usually cry and they are the one who are in the forefront of the battle all the time but for me being at the peace side and clean the mess is another genuine way of being a real hero. I guess I am a bit biased in this case. One of my famous phrases during my young ages was telling how much I admire and deeply are in love with American people (not American politics) simply because of their culture of instilling hope and courage into almost any desperate situation and total despair and disappointment.

One of major characteristic of good business is to show your clients that your mind and heart are aligned, in other words you have integrity. I always say me and Lucy are like soul chiropractor that align mind and souls of ourselves and our clients. The days of corporate pressure to make money by all means have gone and mass public become everyday more conscious of their surroundings and their core values.

We are all trying to make sure serving our customer is in the core of our business model. Sales is the final process but by getting into the mindset to serve, sales become a by product not an agenda. Practice of serving people start by asking good questions, this by itself not only creates an amazing rapport between you and your customer but also is a powerful way of gathering crucial data about your clients to be used later when you are putting all those pieces of puzzles together to come up with a solution and action plan based on the real needs.

The best solution plan is to take your clients desire and expectations to where they wanted to go not to take your promotion and sales quota.

The phenomenon of rejection in your everyday interaction with clients especially in the start which you haven't created a descent book of business is a must go through it story. If you are not properly trained to overcome the awful feeling of being rejected plus proper handling of objections, then it takes a big dent in your business career and a big toll on your psyche.

In our business, we always make it a fun exercise and when we have a new member of the team going from high energy level in the start of the Monday to an absolute desperate dead body at the end of the week then we say the famous phrase: Hey you need a course of rejection therapy and a dose of mental toughness injection!

As an old say "when you face a close door don't push it. In other term don't be a salesy type of personality simply because you've to prove a point. Always try to win quality of your work not your point of conversation.

We all knows about concept of right and left side of the brain, one is super logical and all amenities of critical thinking have been stored there and the other has all the sparkles of creativity and tools for thinking outside of the box to be emotionally involve and present.

Based on that simple schematic there are several personality testing toolboxes that most companies especially at HR and management level use to help them control and use the best of their staff and teammates potentials and use them in their suitable positions and responsibilities.

No matter which one you're using, use something to not put people in boxes and label them but to use them as a powerful tool for their improvement and personal growth in their career path. The worst thing after all those workshops is to use those tools and techniques to further chastise and marginalise people than helping them to grow by giving a twisted version of realty.

In the quest of finding best personality for any position have this in your mind, that always wait to be surprised and amazed about the unbelievable potential of human being for change and transformation.

Reference to all motivational and transformational events which is a multimillion dollar industry and is based both in facts and fiction (depends who is running it and for what purpose) but for a trained mind it's not very difficult to recognise which one to avoid and which one to trust but after some hit and miss (referring to myself attending quite few seminars that barely was tolerate it to stay halfway).

To finish strong, it's highly recommended to work on your fear factor as final recipe for success or failure. When you take your fear factor off of your mind you change your actions to habit.

This is the part that says to overcome your fears it's not enough to know and learn about the topic without jumping all in and make your hand dirty. Action is a prerequisite for transforming your fear into habit as we are all packages of different habits, the more accumulating winning habits like waking up early morning or investing in yourself etc. the more successful we become.

Then if this is the rule now we understand why it says a journey of thousand miles start with one. Action needs consistency and commitment what that is missing in most of early January gym resolutions and why so because most of us stops before any action become a habit as habit are effortless and actions need lots of reasoning and rationalization.

There are different suggestions for time period that changes an action to a habit but minimum is 30 days with no interruption. It doesn't mean that it's a magic number but you may need several 30 days to overcome other adversities which not necessarily connected to laziness and it could be serious health challenges, or valid financial means or family obligation and lots of other legitimate reasons, but remember at the end of the day you are doing for betterment of yourself not anybody else thus lame excuses don't do the justice, then stay away from them. We are talking about tough situations that you want to overcome by getting into your highest mental toughness like a navy seal.

It's simple but it's not easy (reference to most multilevel marketing presentations that they show you the tip of the iceberg with shiny dollar signs but rarely talking about what does it take to get there if by all means have any respect or enthusiasm for MLM business model because I assume all readers have been through one or more kinds of wrong approach by many MLM businesses).

Again, I'm not an specialist in MLM business model analysis but as they are one the main dominant forces out there running giant industry distribution systems in major service areas like health and nutrition, sport enhancement, beauty etc. if you haven't been exposed to any of those presentations behold, because you will!

To explain the concept of Fortune Hand it was a compilation of different ideas and factors that can bring success and fortune into our life especially if you wanted to be an entrepreneur. Why we started with happiness as the first and most important factor to begin with because the energy factor.

As an entrepreneur, you are heading to the outside world with lots of unprepared and unexpected situation that if you are not at your highest state of being it'll drag you down and leave you with a very exhausted and tired aura which subsequently affect the way you deliver your services and interact with clients.

Energy is everything and you are the engineer of the state of mind and responsible for maintenance of your potentials and enthusiasm during the day to make sure you keep it at highest possible state of being. It shows its superior effect when you make a mistake which is inevitable in any action oriented activity.

Talking about attitude when you make a mistake admit it and take full responsibility but don't stop there, you may loss that business but you save your integrity for the hope of make it better next time because it's a proven fact that people change. Acceptance of your mistake have to be acknowledged wholeheartedly and be sincere, otherwise it creates grudges and malfunction in delivering the best services to your clients.

Here is to emphasize the ability to separate your personal emotions and feeling from professional duties which easy to be said but needs lots of practice.

Human brain has wired in a way to take the path of least resistance and simple course of action but to separate professional from personal reaction it takes your brain to work double or triple as usual regarding the amount of efforts it has to put in to make it right.

The issue become more complicated when you have been taught that in the start of any business relationship, making humane and meaningful relationship is the key to success in offering future services to your potential clients. As your professional relationship grow, it has to outgrows your personal side otherwise it'll cause uncomfortable and awkward situation both for you as a service provider and your customer.

As you work on your relationship terms like integrity and respect will show up quite frequently and you have to consider the fact that growth and maturity of your relationship is a process and not a sudden event.

When you are offering a service as act of serving people's need based on law of attraction it means: from factual and pragmatic approach point of view whatever you put out there good or bad, eventually will get back to you 10 folds' as return of your investment. The reason behind this discrepancy is that we are not aware of all known and unknown sources that you would considered in the first when it comes to cause and effect.

Thus, when we offer a service we do it with our outmost care and positive intention like this is the first and last time we have the opportunity to serve this client.

Another fact that explain why to believe in law of attraction and implement it in your daily business is the factor of control which most of us love to have %100 in all steps of our business but in reality, is a rarity why because there are lots of external factors that can turn around the situation you have bee planned to act and do business in. This is called fake sense of having control over the whole process which creates a lot of tension and stress when things go sideways and not in order that we thought supposed to.

The main reason why most of us get stuck into the concept of control is because of another rule which has been taught as the crucial factor for success so called "being crystal focus on a target". This by itself creates a false sense of full control and confidence. Those 2 forces of being crystal clear focus on the target and at the same time having flexibility of dancing with the external influences can be a cause of confusion and blur the line between when to say no to a client or fire a client.

Concept of finding your tribe and in case of using it for your client so called finding your "avatar" is a testimony that not all business interactions can end to a result we were expecting. Having this in mind gauge our expectations to a more realistic level and help us move on faster when deals are not reached based on our assumptions.

Continuing in our Fortune Hand infographic the 2nd factor in creating success is having the courage to move and to change based on new circumstances.

Courage moves and is the engine behind breaking the status quo. For you to pump up your courage there is an old rule of face your pain and face your gain. By default, we are procrastinators being, and pain is the major force behind most of our courageous act that otherwise we wouldn't have been taken action in a normal circumstance.

Facing your pain and fear of loss is the traditional driving force, behind most sales pith presentations to convince you that if you don't act today you're losing big time or in another word "tomorrow is late".

This is more of a pressure tactic but if we look at last minute tax submission or study for exam or flight check in or time management struggles or lousy excuses for not being fully prepared, all are having some roots in human procrastination tendency.

Historically scare tactic has been playing major roles in military structure or heavy duty industries that demands an extra ordinary level of precision and attention to details. Otherwise it creates chaos and failures but its implementation has been trickled down to our daily routines and for sure to our business decision making.

But what has been a main driving force in precision and being in action mode constantly, can create exhaustion and burn out in a journey of entrepreneurship. When your both professional and personal life are at stake and you're responsible to pull them off and put your things together, most of the time at least in early stage of your business growth, just the inability to adjust your working hours and rest of your human needs and responsibilities can steer you away from the balance and destroy your Business if not your life.

The more mature you'll get in your motivation for action (just do it phase) the more "gain" (in contrast to pain and fear) will become the driving force behind all of activities including your business. Fear, can move a nation but joy and positivity, will create a sustainable foundation for change and growth.

The 3rd factor in Fortune hand is your confidence. To be confident you've to acquire a certain level of knowledge and skills that industry standards require by ways of getting license, CE credits, continuing professional development, ongoing mentorship, onsite training's and so on. The biggest surprise will pop up when you involve participants in simple self help tools like elevator pitch or 30 seconds' presentation. No matter how much it looks cheesy and salesy but at the same time it's a fairly quick test that shows your level of clarity and understanding of where are you at and what kind of values you are delivering to your client.

Last but not least is the 5th factor of having mentors. No matter what degree or academic qualifications you've achieved, the ability to get access to high quality mentors who have proven records of practice and expertise and the one who are using a model that resonate with your core values and standards is the last step toward making a successful action plan for success. Most of us for sure have to go through a big battle of crushing our heavy invested ego to overcome the fear and anxiety of reaching out to amazing mentors but if we do it right and we do it early in our business it saves us lots of time, pain, energy and dollars.

www.ingramcontent.com/pod-product-compliance
Lightning Source LLC
Chambersburg PA
CBHW071831200526
45169CB00018B/1320